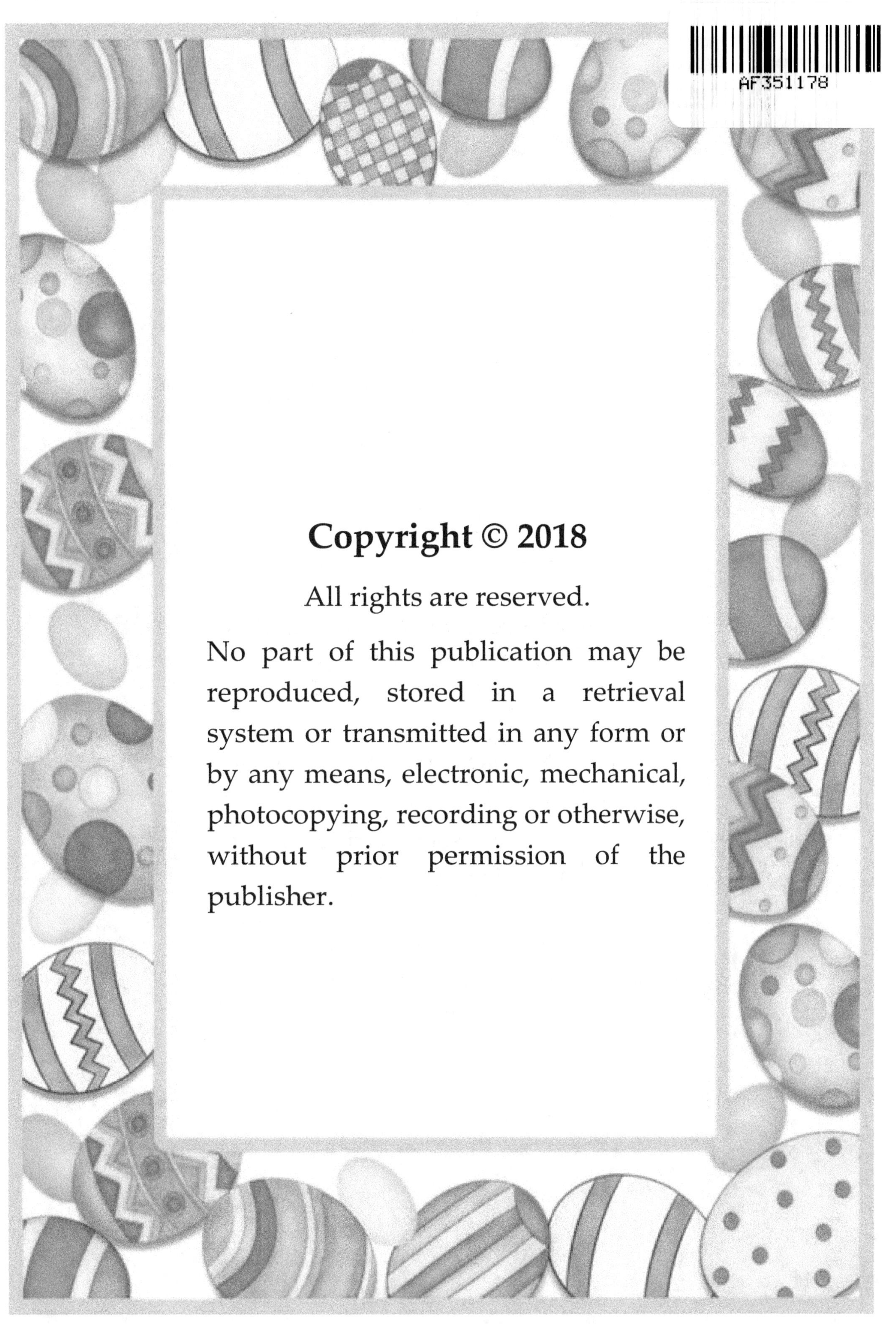

Copyright © 2018

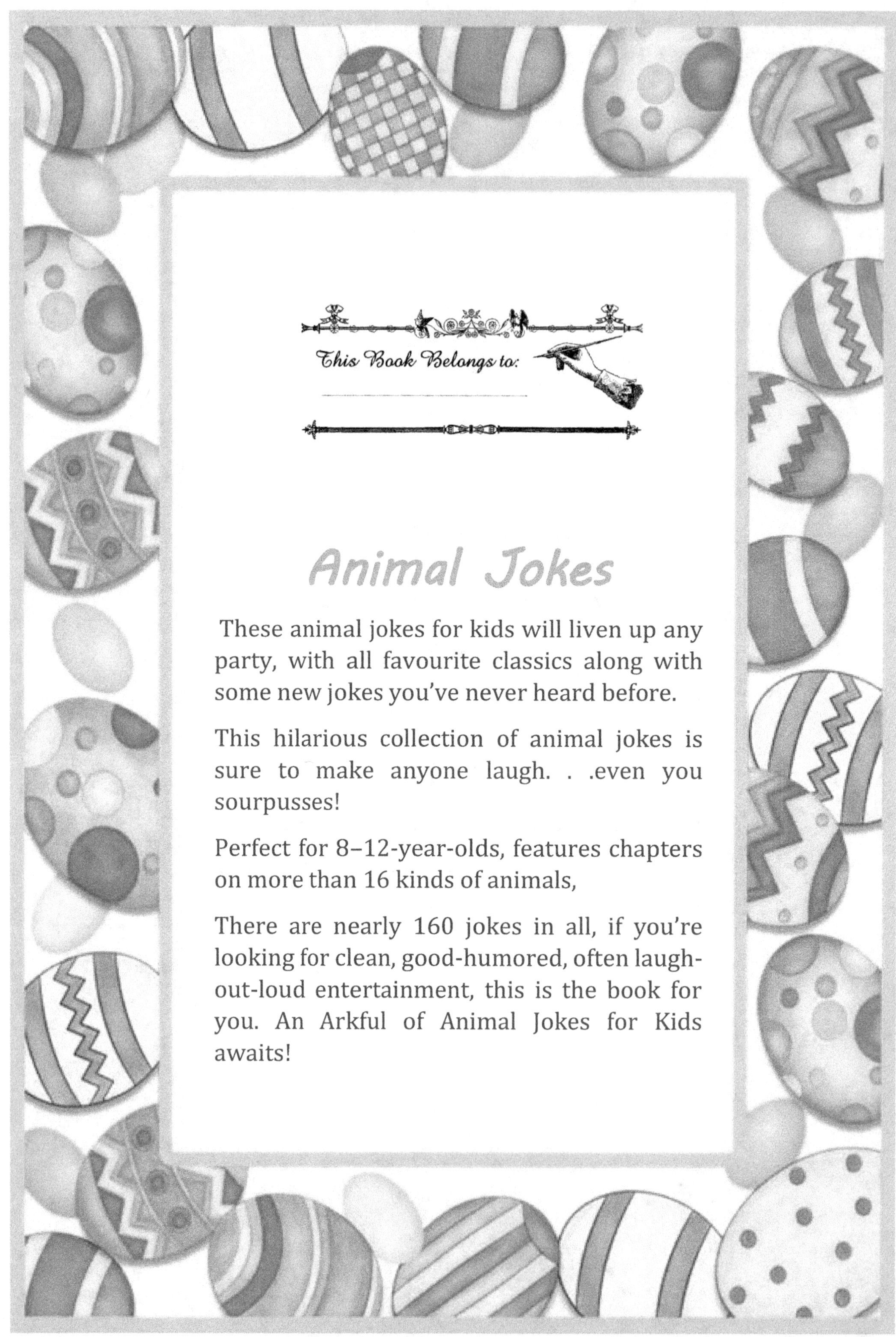

Animal Jokes

These animal jokes for kids will liven up any party, with all favourite classics along with some new jokes you've never heard before.

This hilarious collection of animal jokes is sure to make anyone laugh. . .even you sourpusses!

Perfect for 8–12-year-olds, features chapters on more than 16 kinds of animals,

There are nearly 160 jokes in all, if you're looking for clean, good-humored, often laugh-out-loud entertainment, this is the book for you. An Arkful of Animal Jokes for Kids awaits!

Elephant Jokes

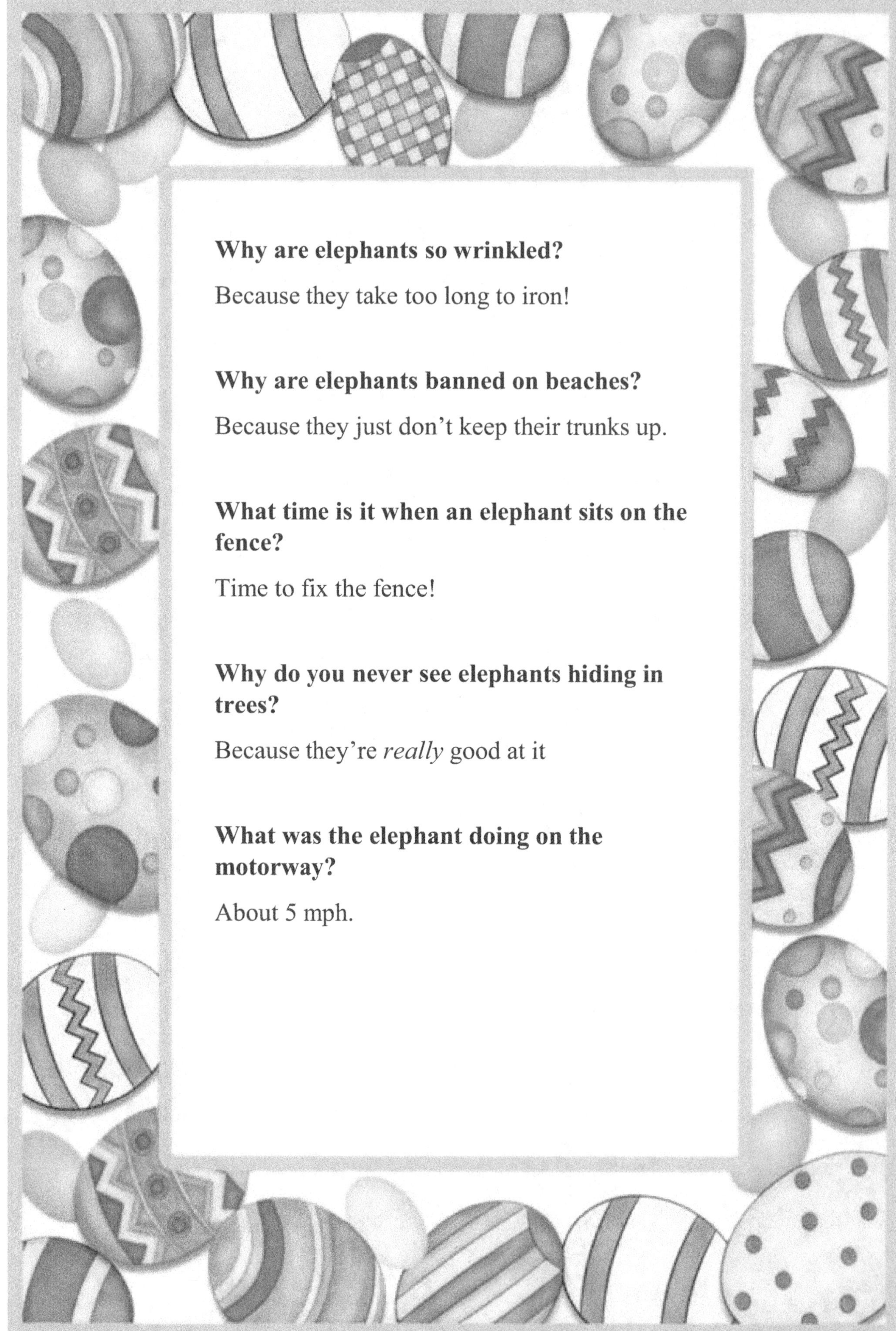

Why are elephants so wrinkled?

Because they take too long to iron!

Why are elephants banned on beaches?

Because they just don't keep their trunks up.

What time is it when an elephant sits on the fence?

Time to fix the fence!

Why do you never see elephants hiding in trees?

Because they're *really* good at it

What was the elephant doing on the motorway?

About 5 mph.

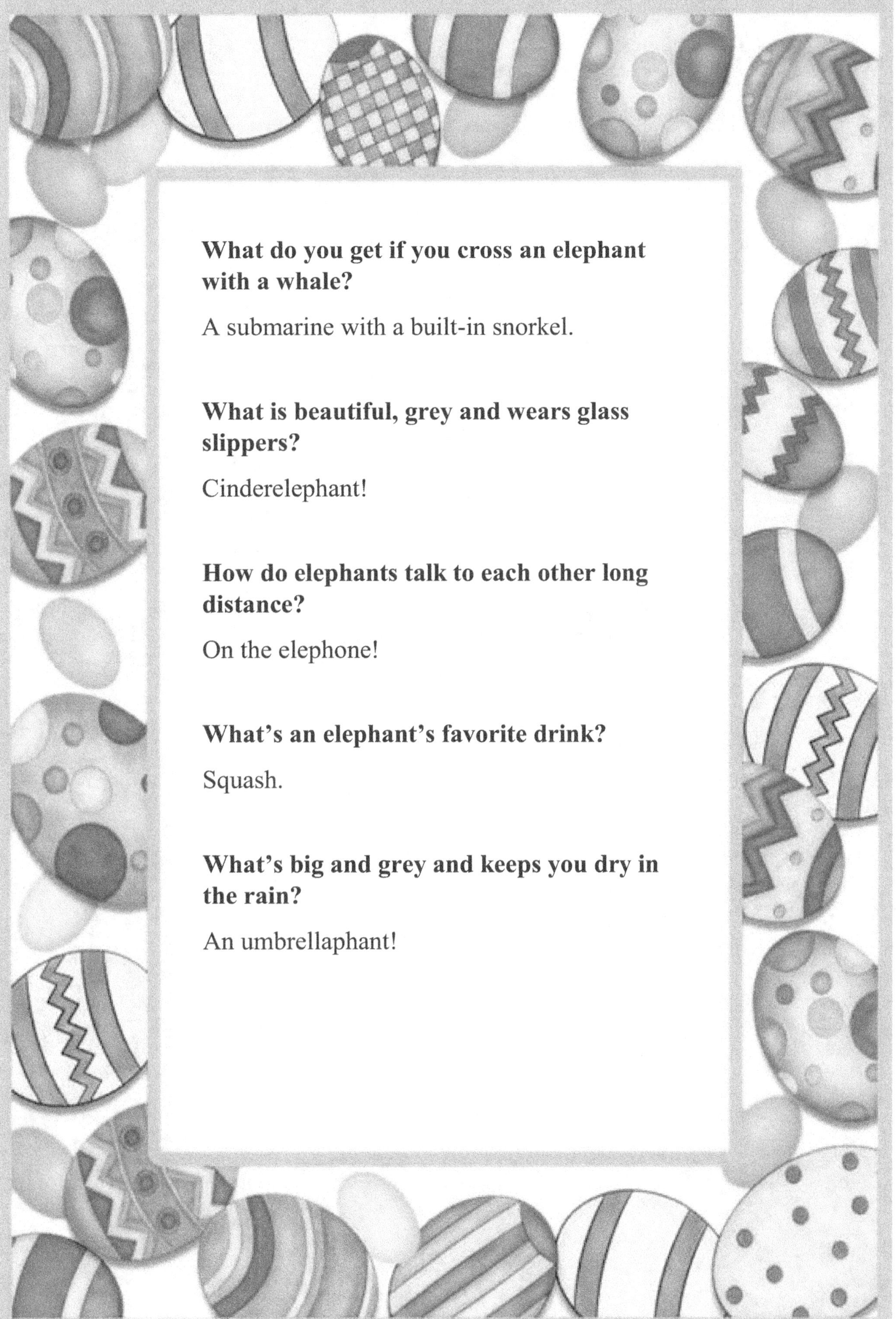

What do you get if you cross an elephant with a whale?

A submarine with a built-in snorkel.

What is beautiful, grey and wears glass slippers?

Cinderelephant!

How do elephants talk to each other long distance?

On the elephone!

What's an elephant's favorite drink?

Squash.

What's big and grey and keeps you dry in the rain?

An umbrellaphant!

Fish Jokes

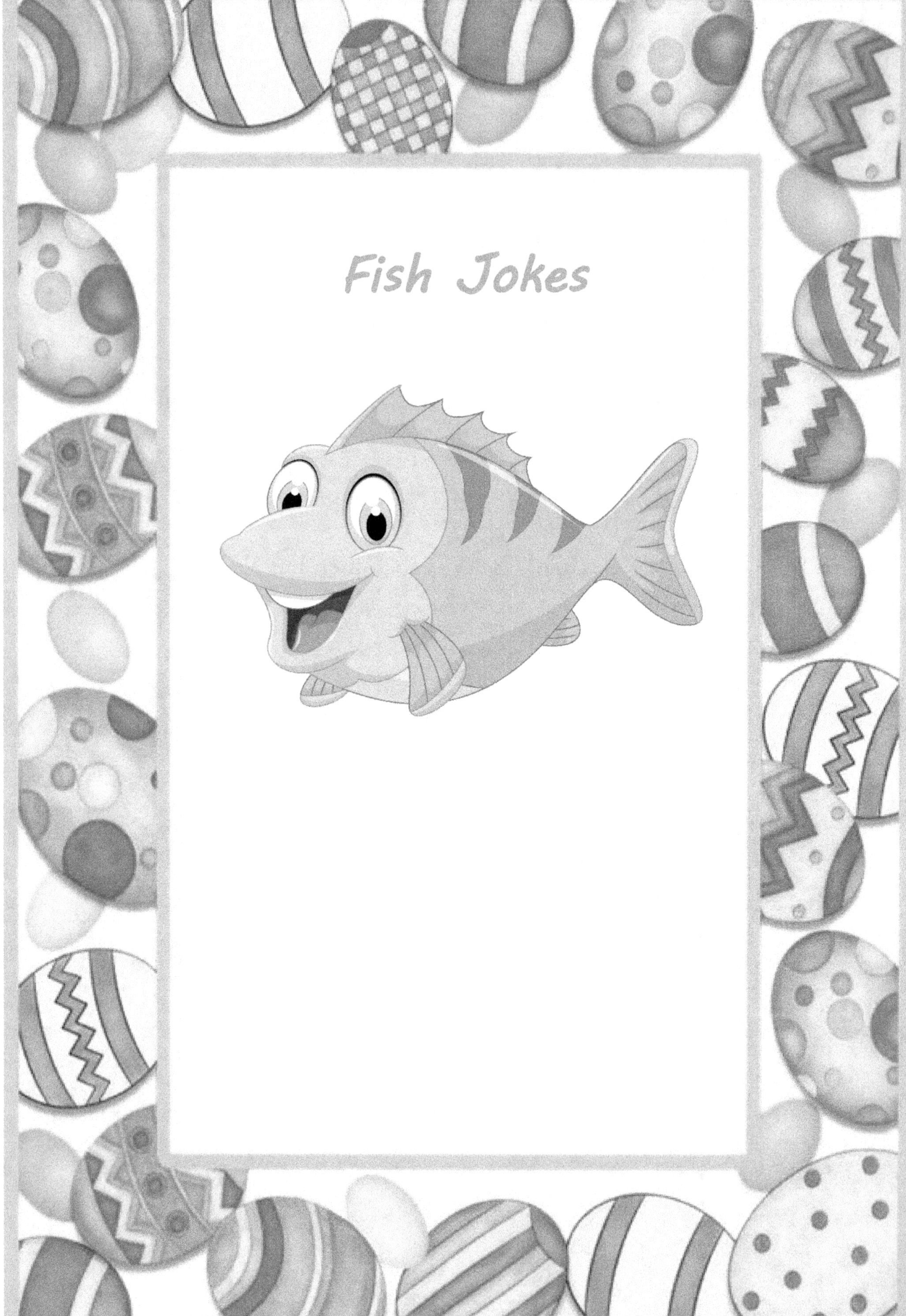

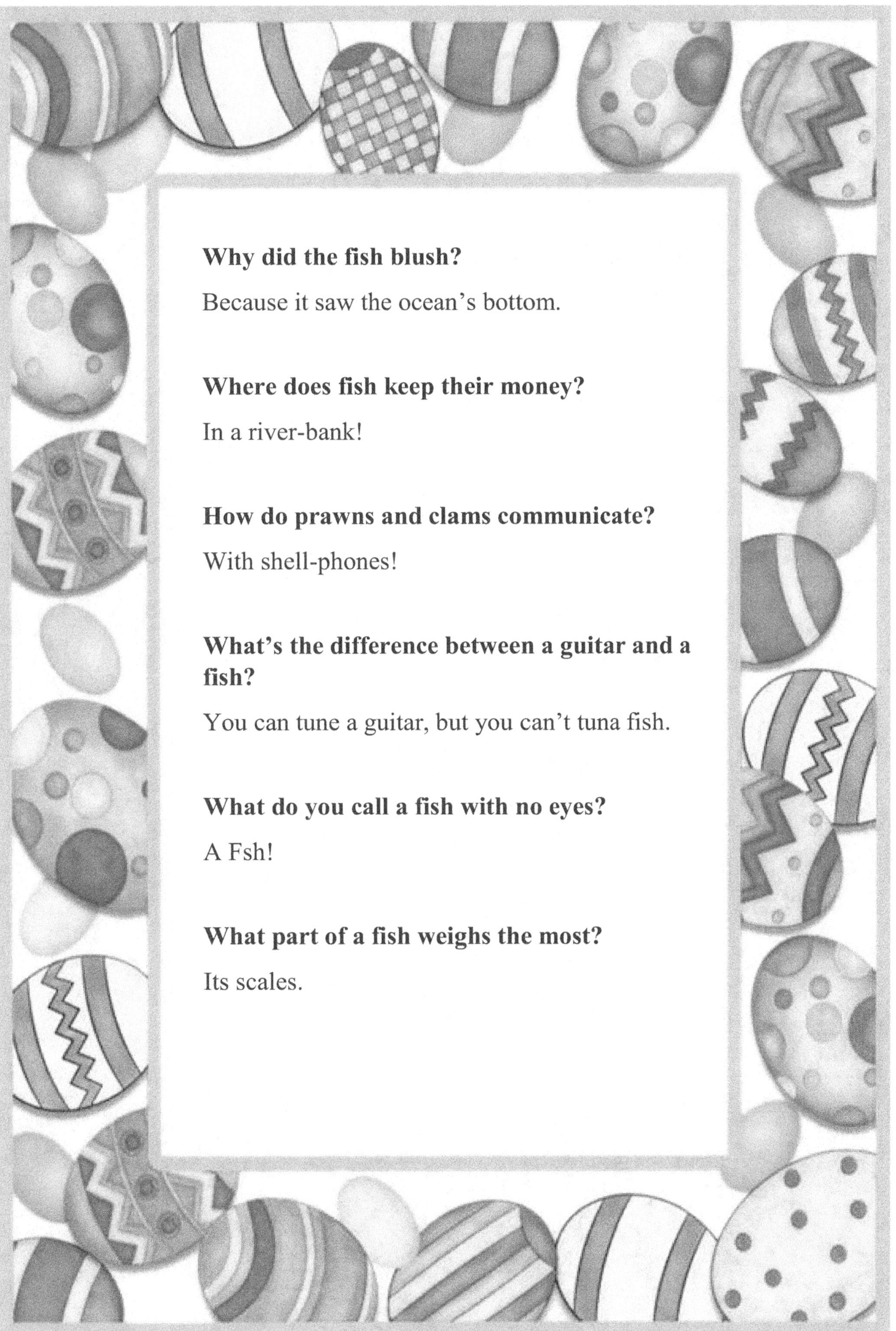

Why did the fish blush?

Because it saw the ocean's bottom.

Where does fish keep their money?

In a river-bank!

How do prawns and clams communicate?

With shell-phones!

What's the difference between a guitar and a fish?

You can tune a guitar, but you can't tuna fish.

What do you call a fish with no eyes?

A Fsh!

What part of a fish weighs the most?

Its scales.

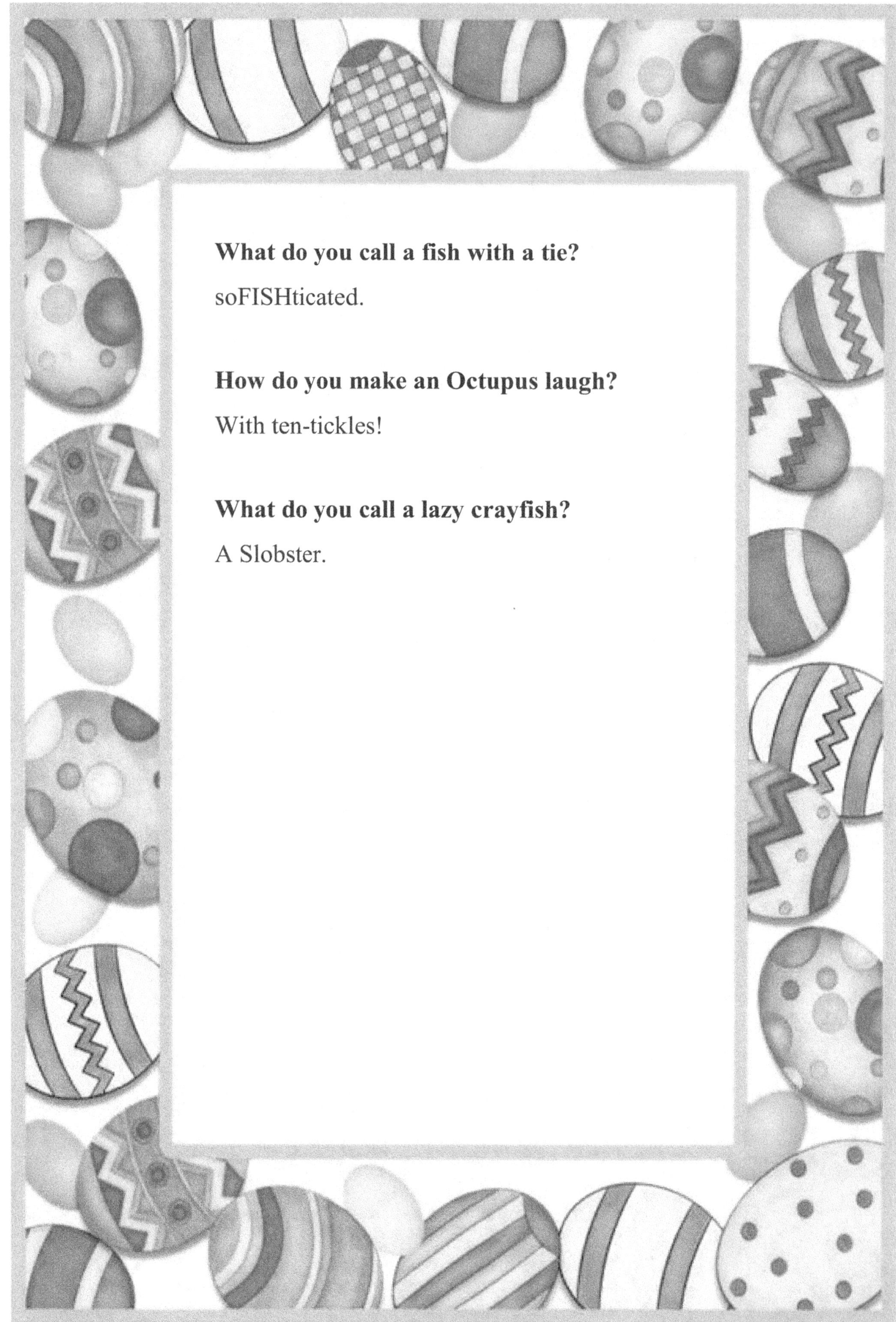

What do you call a fish with a tie?

soFISHticated.

How do you make an Octupus laugh?

With ten-tickles!

What do you call a lazy crayfish?

A Slobster.

Chicken Jokes

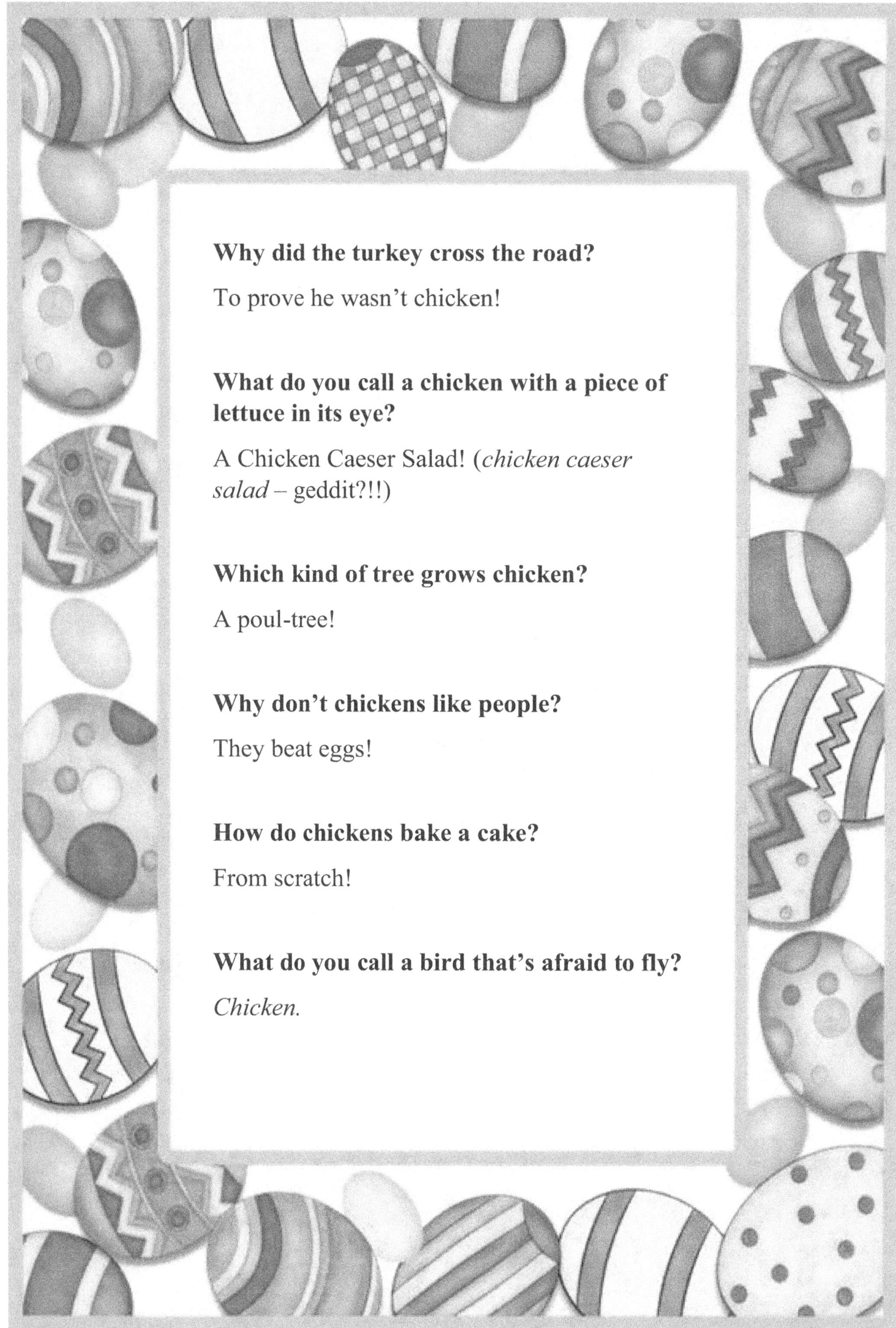

Why did the turkey cross the road?

To prove he wasn't chicken!

What do you call a chicken with a piece of lettuce in its eye?

A Chicken Caeser Salad! (*chicken caeser salad* – geddit?!!)

Which kind of tree grows chicken?

A poul-tree!

Why don't chickens like people?

They beat eggs!

How do chickens bake a cake?

From scratch!

What do you call a bird that's afraid to fly?

Chicken.

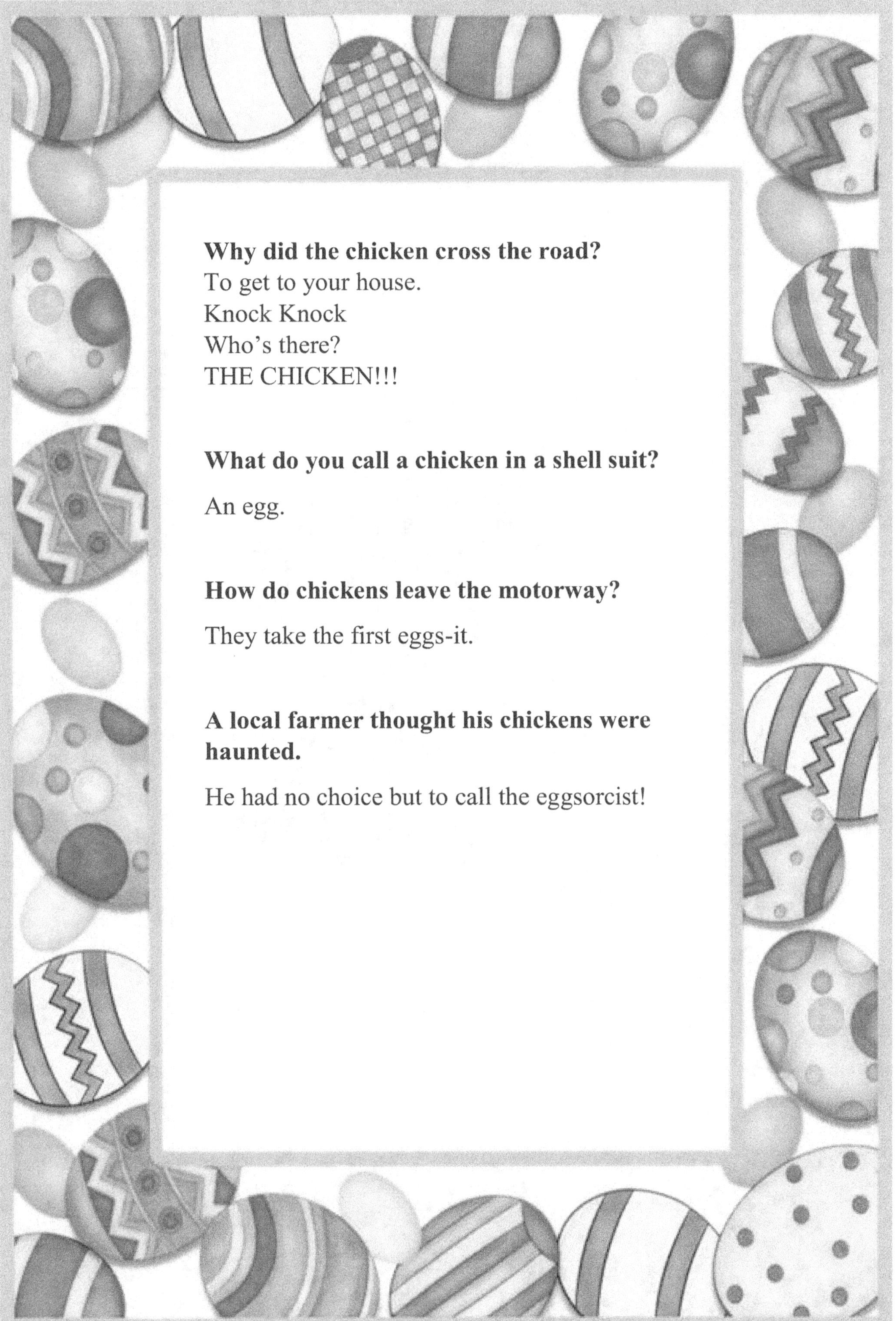

Why did the chicken cross the road?
To get to your house.
Knock Knock
Who's there?
THE CHICKEN!!!

What do you call a chicken in a shell suit?

An egg.

How do chickens leave the motorway?

They take the first eggs-it.

A local farmer thought his chickens were haunted.

He had no choice but to call the eggsorcist!

Dog Jokes

Why do dogs run in circles?

Because its hard to run in squares!

What do you get when you cross a dog and a calculator?

A friend you can count on.

What is a dogs favorite instrument?

A trombone.

My dog's got no nose.
How does he smell?
Awful!

What does a dog say before eating?

Bone appetite!

How does a dog stop a TV show?

He presses paws!

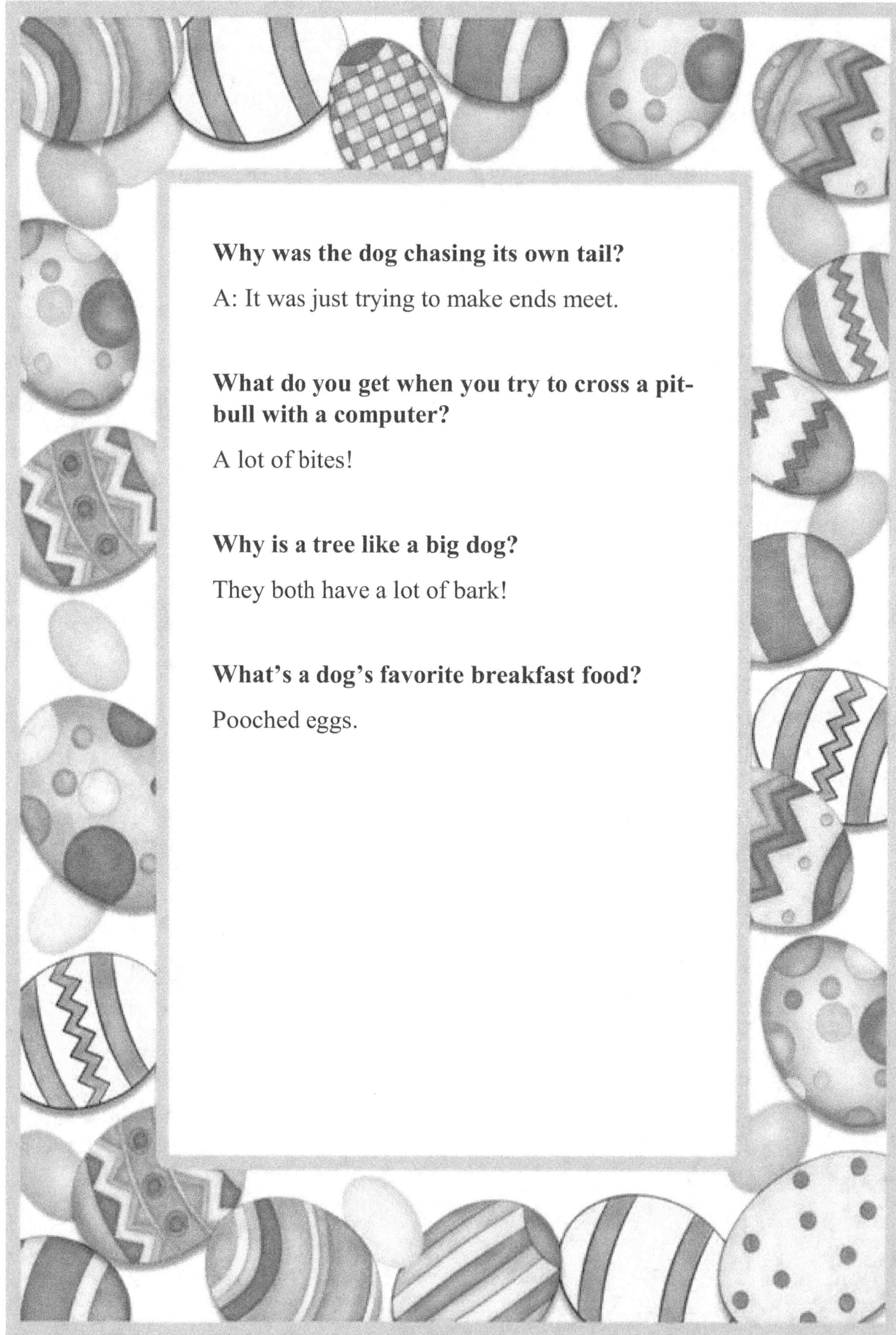

Why was the dog chasing its own tail?

A: It was just trying to make ends meet.

What do you get when you try to cross a pit-bull with a computer?

A lot of bites!

Why is a tree like a big dog?

They both have a lot of bark!

What's a dog's favorite breakfast food?

Pooched eggs.

Cat Jokes

What do you call a cat that lives in an igloo?

An eskimew!

What happened when the cat ate a ball of wool?

She had mittens!

Why don't cats like online shopping?

They prefer to use a cat-alogue.

What is a cat's favorite car?

A Catillac!

What did the cat say when he ran out of money?

I'm paw!

What do you get if you cross a cat with a parrot?

A carrot!

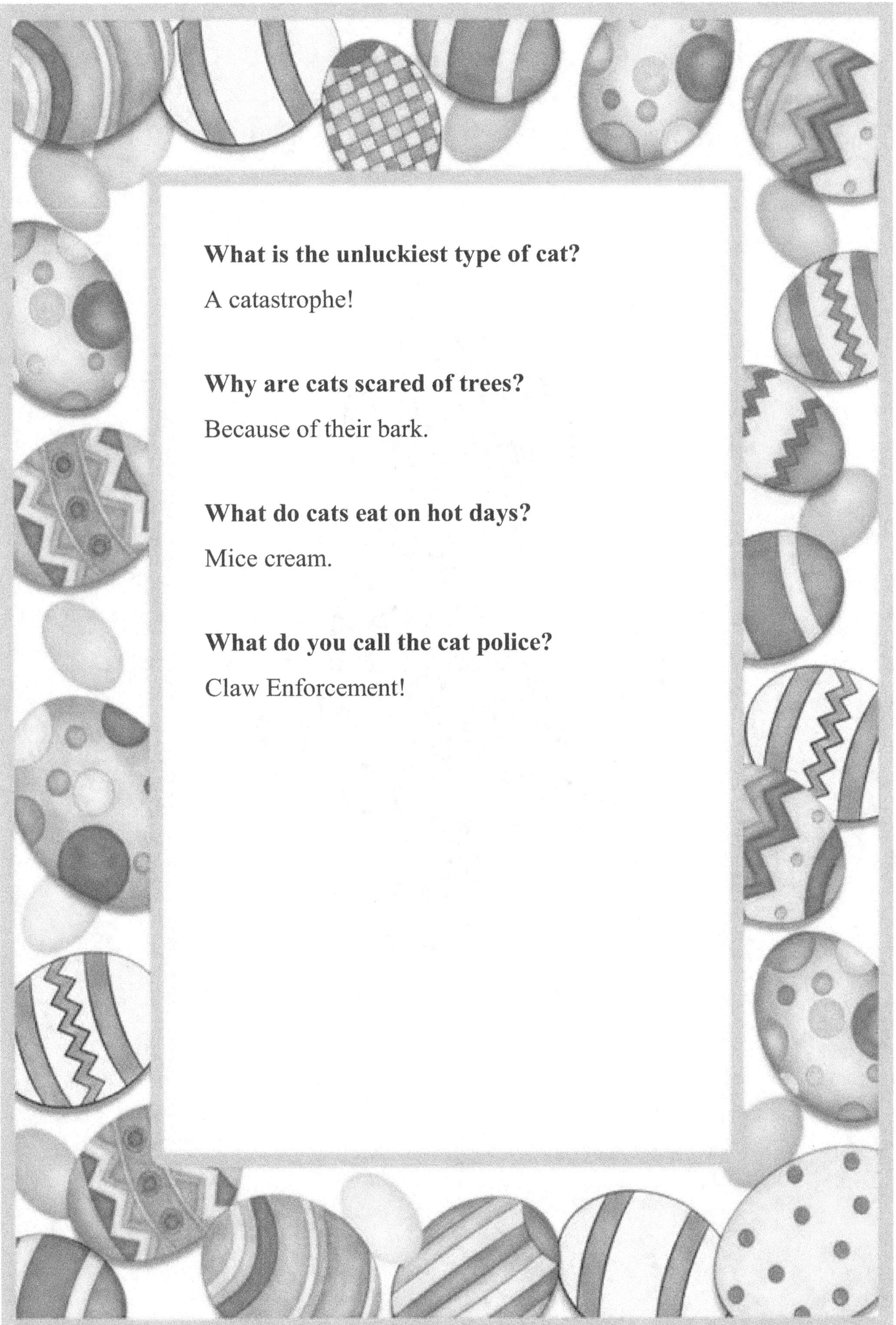

What is the unluckiest type of cat?

A catastrophe!

Why are cats scared of trees?

Because of their bark.

What do cats eat on hot days?

Mice cream.

What do you call the cat police?

Claw Enforcement!

Duck Jokes

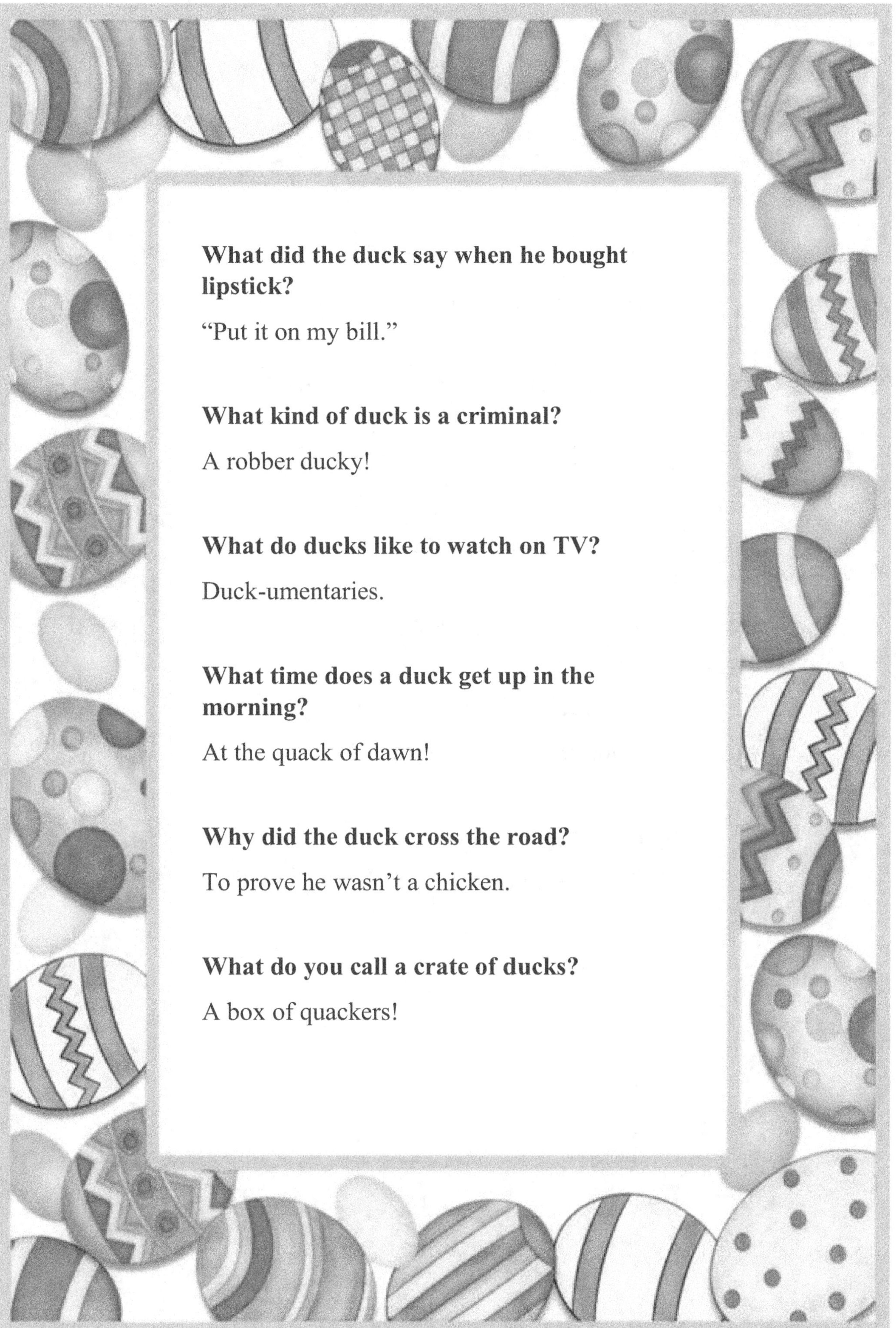

What did the duck say when he bought lipstick?

"Put it on my bill."

What kind of duck is a criminal?

A robber ducky!

What do ducks like to watch on TV?

Duck-umentaries.

What time does a duck get up in the morning?

At the quack of dawn!

Why did the duck cross the road?

To prove he wasn't a chicken.

What do you call a crate of ducks?

A box of quackers!

Why did the dog chase the duck?

Because everyone kept telling him to get down.

How do you make a duck sing beautiful soul music?

Put him in the microwave until his Bill Withers.

Did you hear about the duck who thought he was a squirrel?

It was one tough nut to crack!

Why are ducks really bad at driving?

Their windscreens are all quacked!

What says 'Quick, Quick!'?

A duck with the hiccups.

Bird Jokes

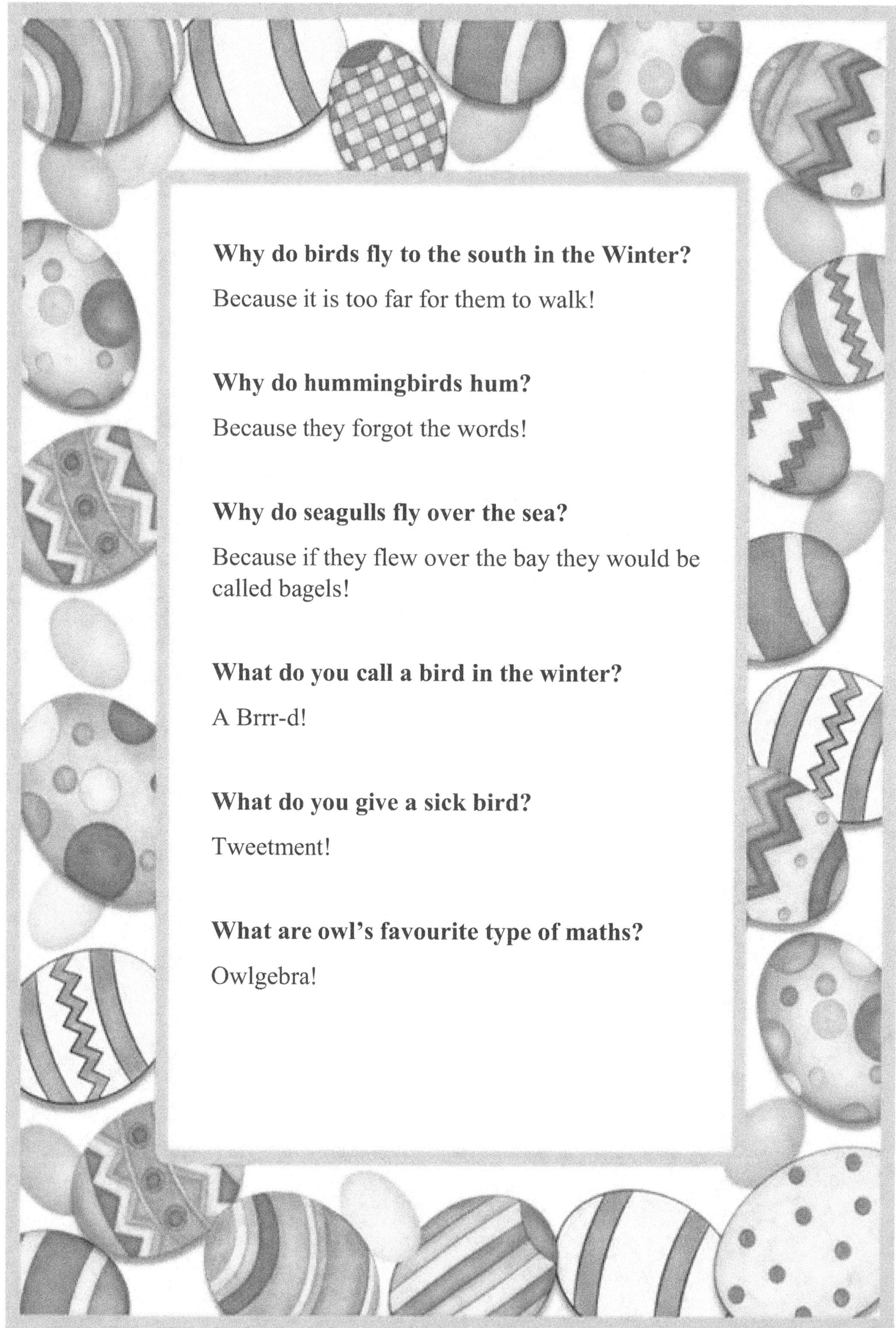

Why do birds fly to the south in the Winter?

Because it is too far for them to walk!

Why do hummingbirds hum?

Because they forgot the words!

Why do seagulls fly over the sea?

Because if they flew over the bay they would be called bagels!

What do you call a bird in the winter?

A Brrr-d!

What do you give a sick bird?

Tweetment!

What are owl's favourite type of maths?

Owlgebra!

Which bird is always out of breath?

A puffin!

How did the bird break into the house?

With a crow bar!

Why did the pelican get kicked out of the restaurant?

He had a big bill.

What do you get when you cross a bird with a lawnmower?

Shredded Tweet.

Pig Jokes

What do you call a pig that does karate?

A pork chop.

What is a pig's favourite colour?

MaHOGany!

Why should you never tell a pig a secret?

They always squeal!

What do pigs use when they are ill?

Oinkment.

How do pigs write secret messages?

With invisible oink!

Why couldn't the pug tie his shoelaces?

He was too ham-fisted!

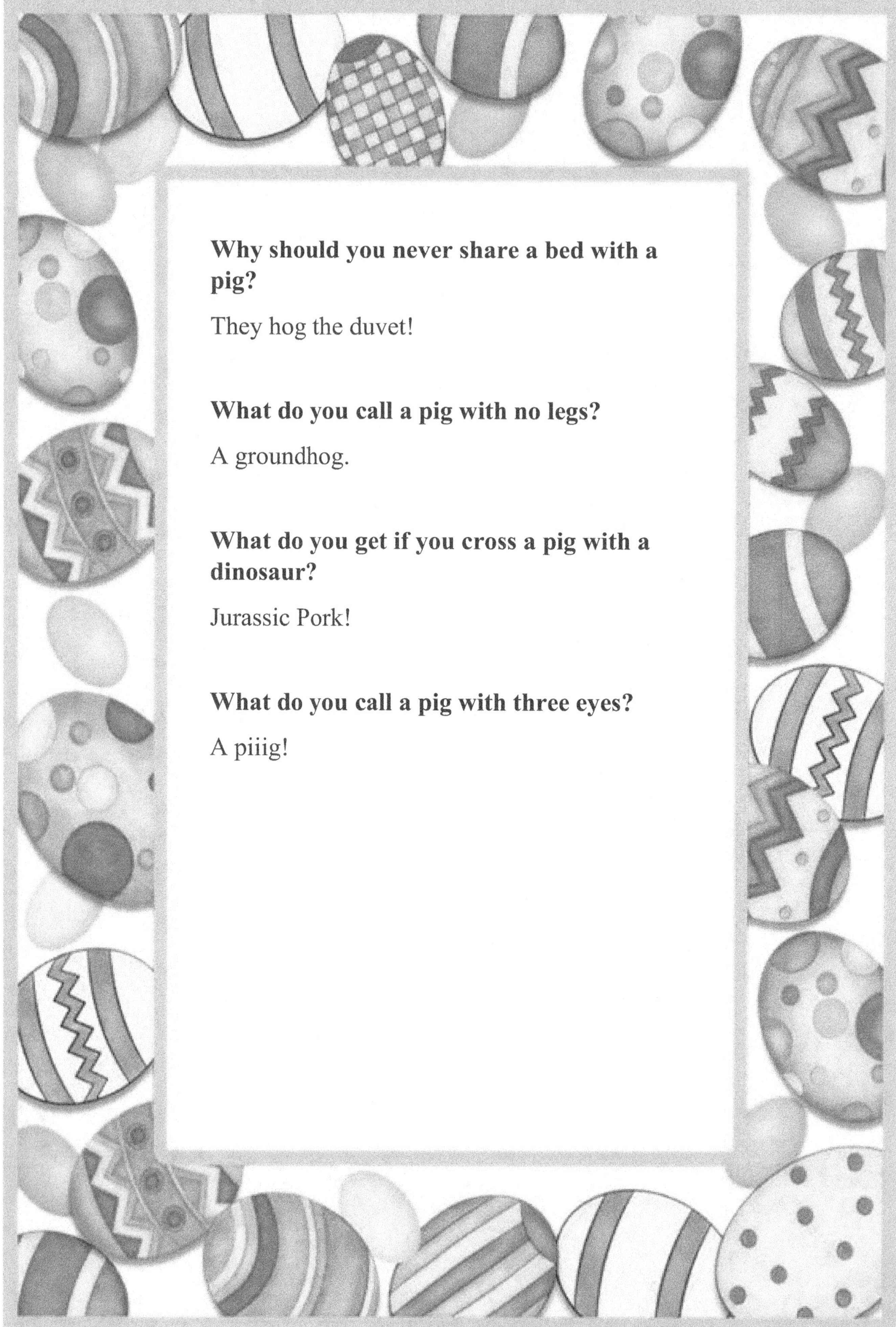

Why should you never share a bed with a pig?

They hog the duvet!

What do you call a pig with no legs?

A groundhog.

What do you get if you cross a pig with a dinosaur?

Jurassic Pork!

What do you call a pig with three eyes?

A piiig!

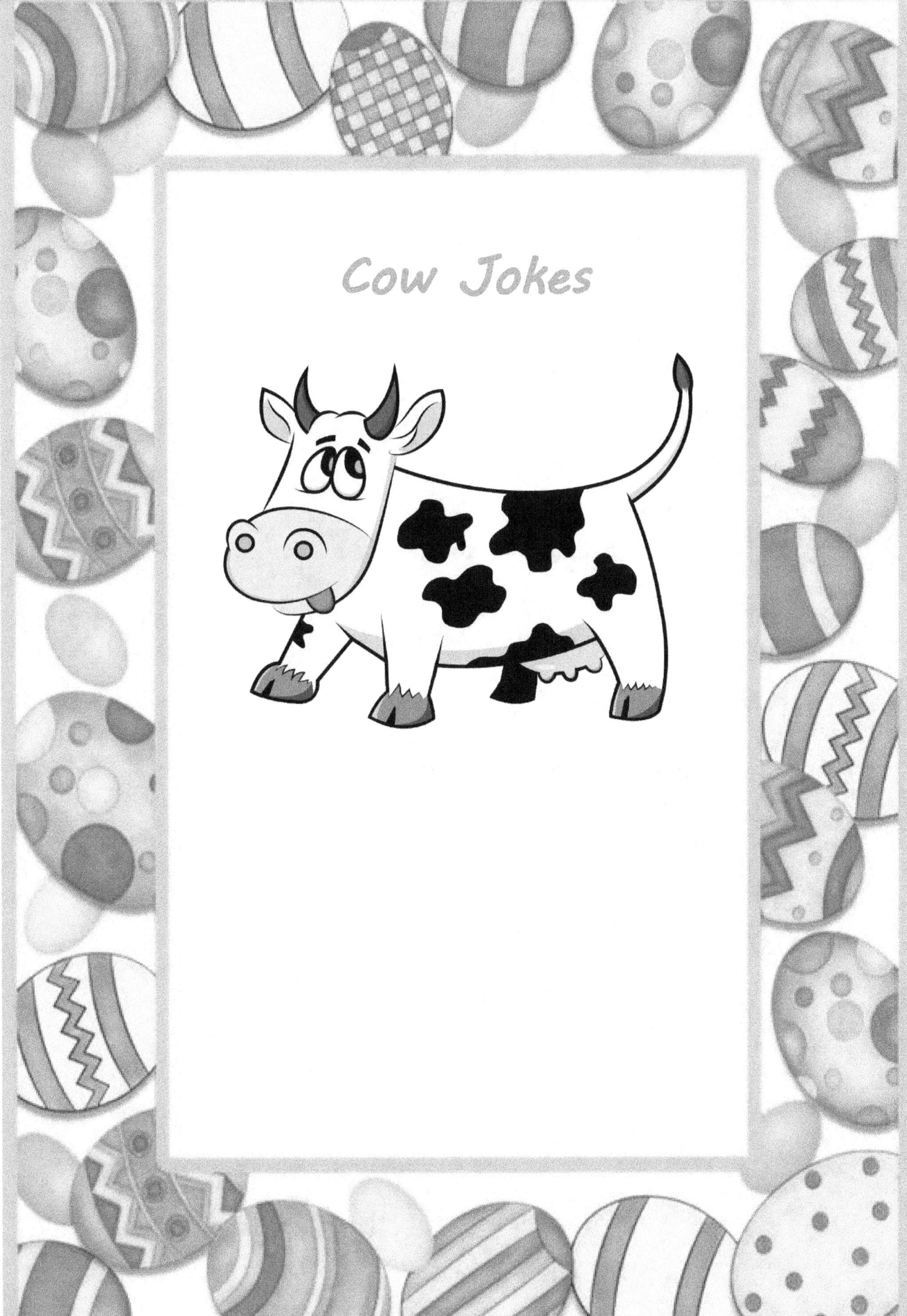
Cow Jokes

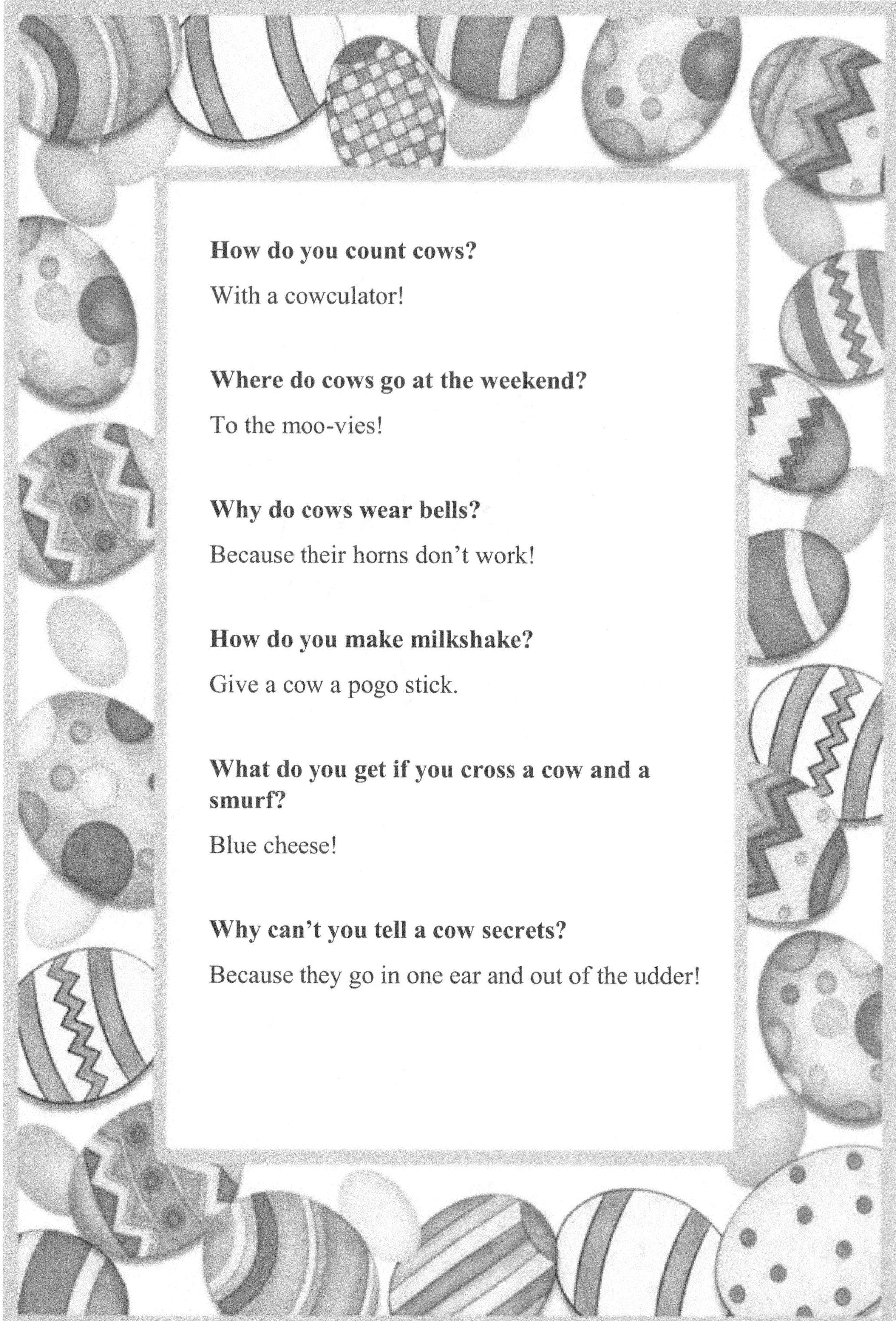

How do you count cows?

With a cowculator!

Where do cows go at the weekend?

To the moo-vies!

Why do cows wear bells?

Because their horns don't work!

How do you make milkshake?

Give a cow a pogo stick.

What do you get if you cross a cow and a smurf?

Blue cheese!

Why can't you tell a cow secrets?

Because they go in one ear and out of the udder!

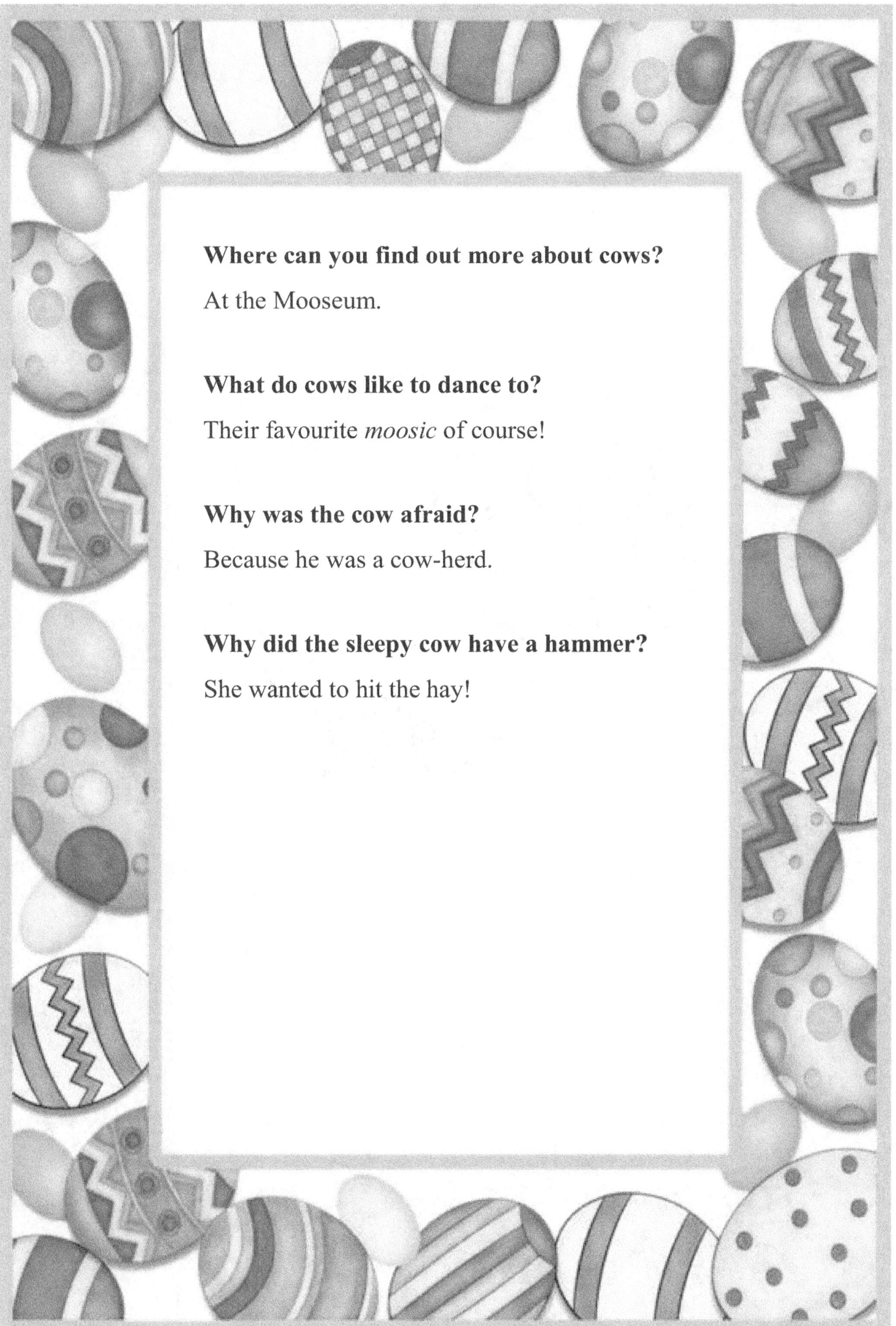

Where can you find out more about cows?

At the Mooseum.

What do cows like to dance to?

Their favourite *moosic* of course!

Why was the cow afraid?

Because he was a cow-herd.

Why did the sleepy cow have a hammer?

She wanted to hit the hay!

Sheep Jokes

What's a sheep's favourite game?

Baa – dminton!

What did one sheep say to the other?

After ewe!

What do you call a sheep with no legs?

A cloud.

Why are sheep considered to be bad drivers?

They are rubbish at ewe-turns!

Where do sheep go on holiday?

To the Baaaaaa-hamas!

What do you call a dancing sheep?

A baa-lerina.

What's a sheep's favourite snack?

A chocolate baa-r!

A sheep, drum and a snake fall off a cliff.

Baa-Dum-Tssssss!!!

Where do sheeps wash?

In the baaaaath tub!

What do sheep sing at Christmas?

Merry Christmas To Ewe!

Horse Jokes

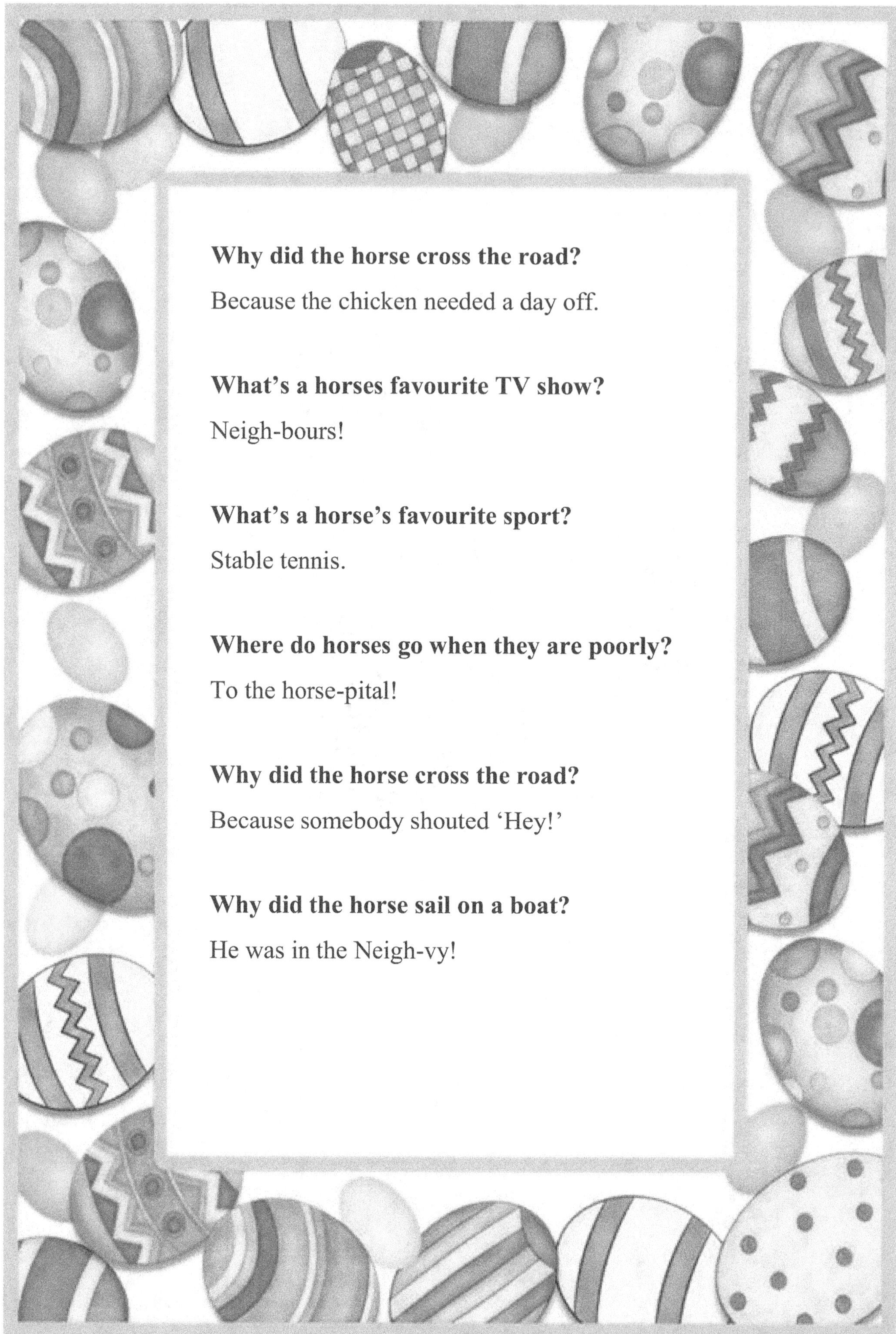

Why did the horse cross the road?

Because the chicken needed a day off.

What's a horses favourite TV show?

Neigh-bours!

What's a horse's favourite sport?

Stable tennis.

Where do horses go when they are poorly?

To the horse-pital!

Why did the horse cross the road?

Because somebody shouted 'Hey!'

Why did the horse sail on a boat?

He was in the Neigh-vy!

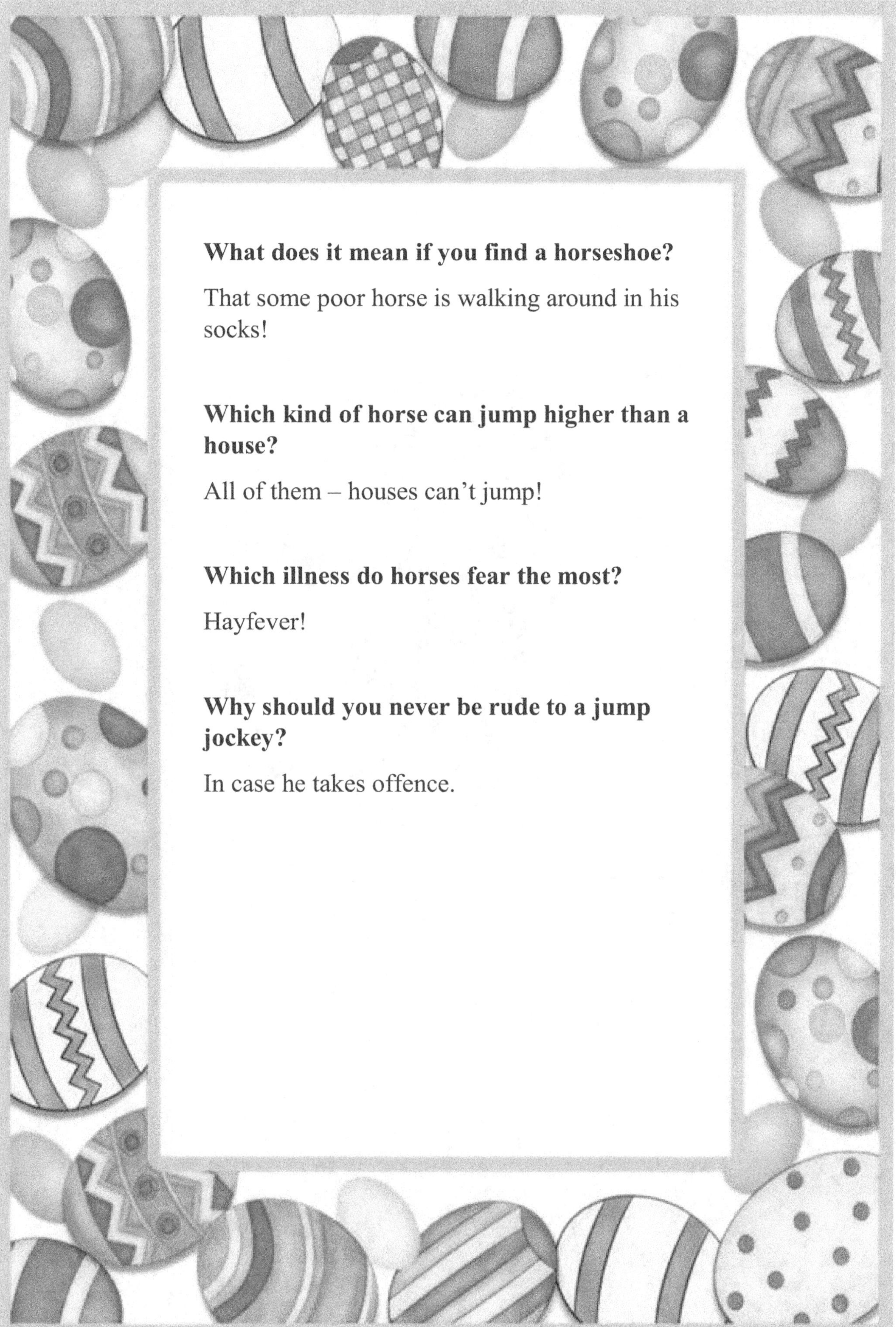

What does it mean if you find a horseshoe?

That some poor horse is walking around in his socks!

Which kind of horse can jump higher than a house?

All of them – houses can't jump!

Which illness do horses fear the most?

Hayfever!

Why should you never be rude to a jump jockey?

In case he takes offence.

Monkey Jokes

Where should a monkey go when he loses his tail?

To a retailer!

What do you call a monkey in a minefield?

A Baboom!

What do monkeys wear when cooking?

Ape-rons!

Why do gorillas have such big nostrils?

Because they have big fingers!

What do you call an exploding monkey?

A bab-oom!

What kind of monkey flies through the air?

A hot air baboon!

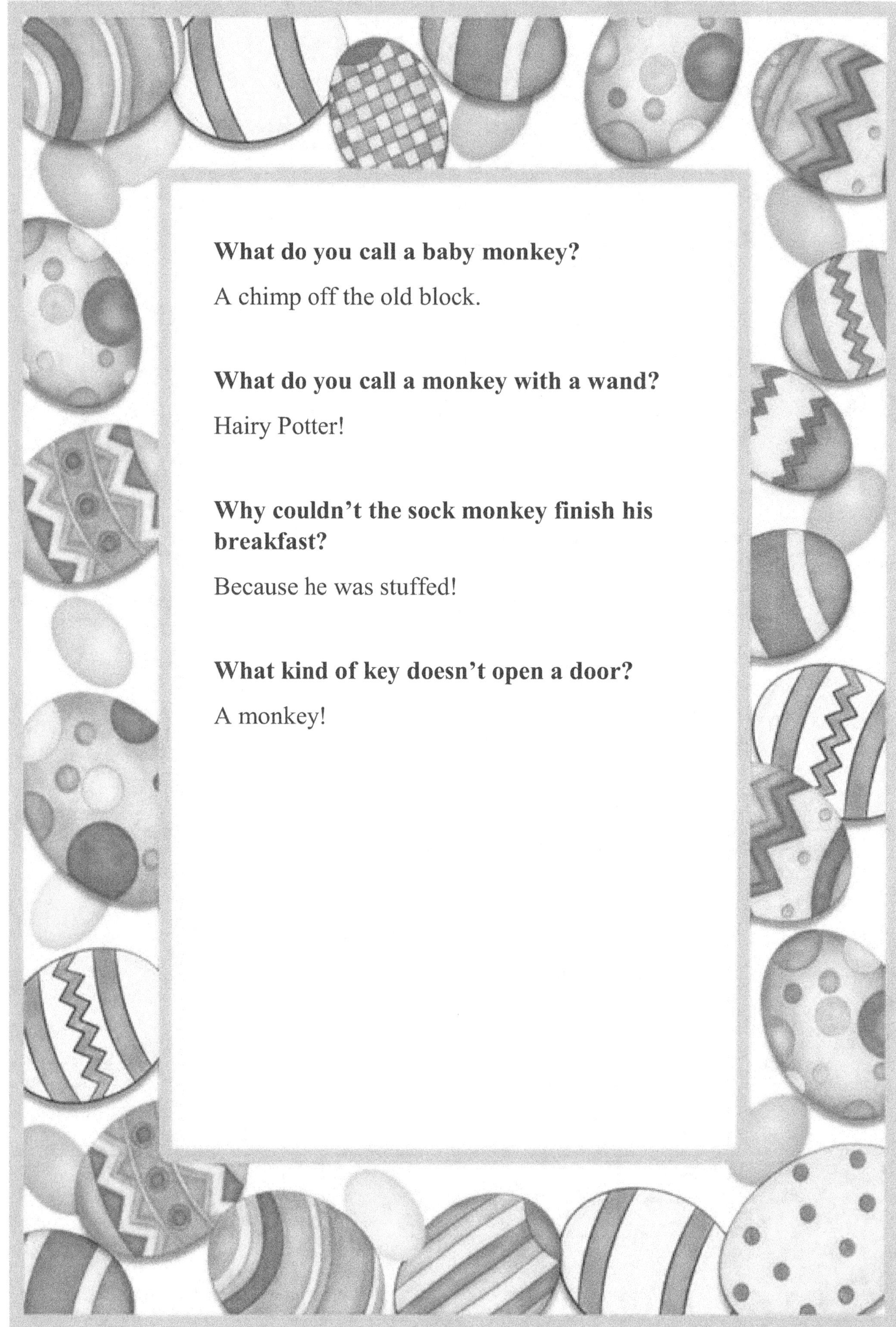

What do you call a baby monkey?

A chimp off the old block.

What do you call a monkey with a wand?

Hairy Potter!

Why couldn't the sock monkey finish his breakfast?

Because he was stuffed!

What kind of key doesn't open a door?

A monkey!

Lion Jokes

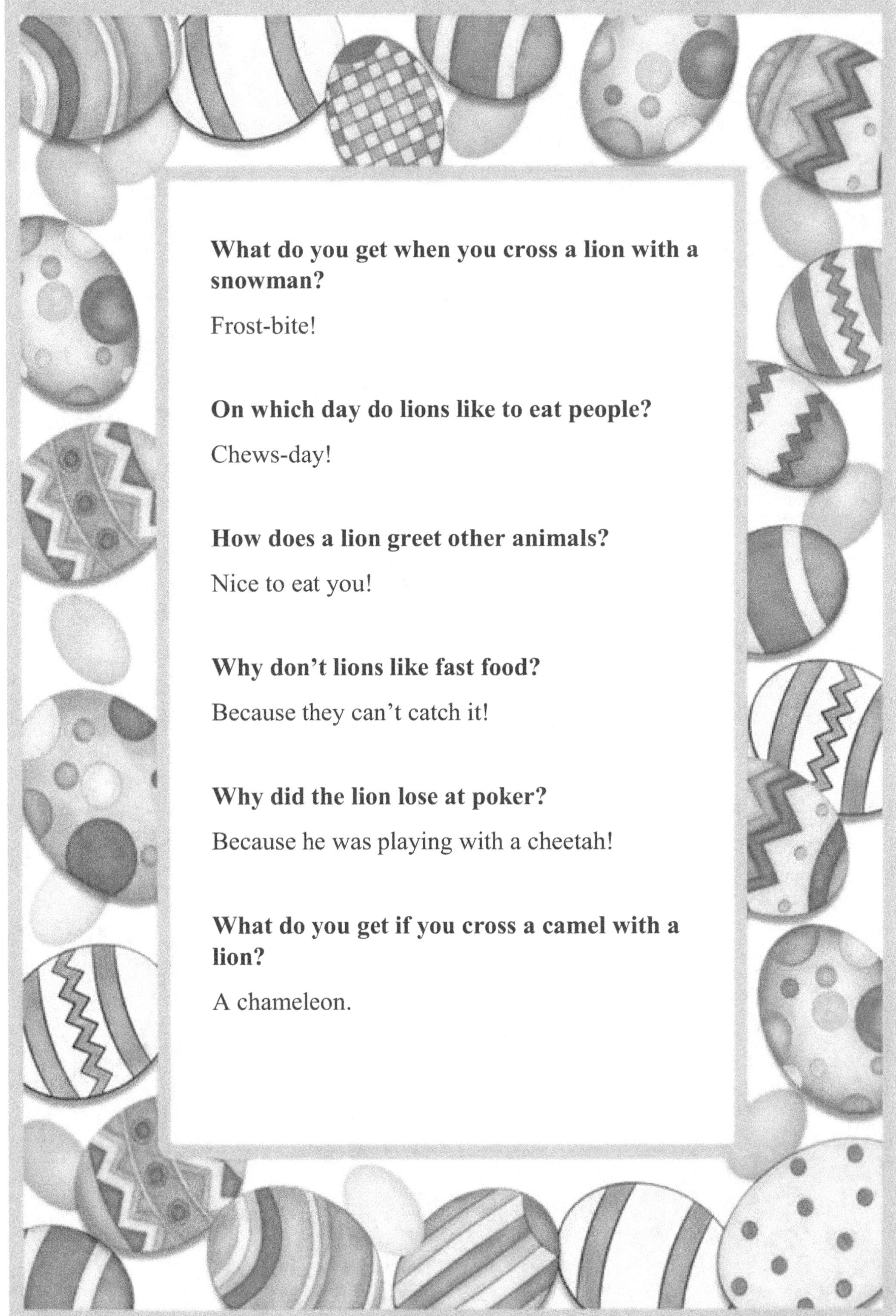

What do you get when you cross a lion with a snowman?

Frost-bite!

On which day do lions like to eat people?

Chews-day!

How does a lion greet other animals?

Nice to eat you!

Why don't lions like fast food?

Because they can't catch it!

Why did the lion lose at poker?

Because he was playing with a cheetah!

What do you get if you cross a camel with a lion?

A chameleon.

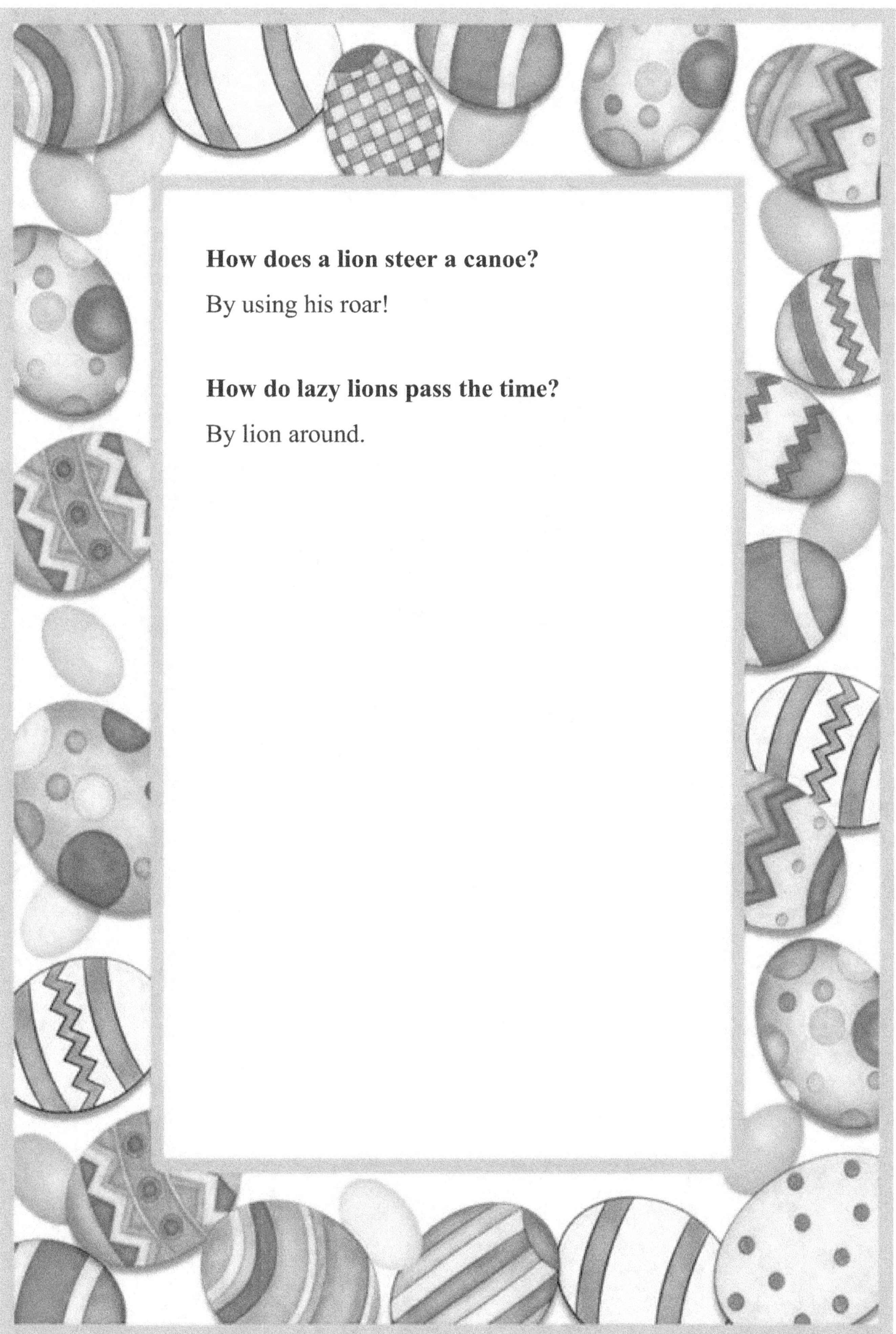

How does a lion steer a canoe?

By using his roar!

How do lazy lions pass the time?

By lion around.

Tiger Jokes

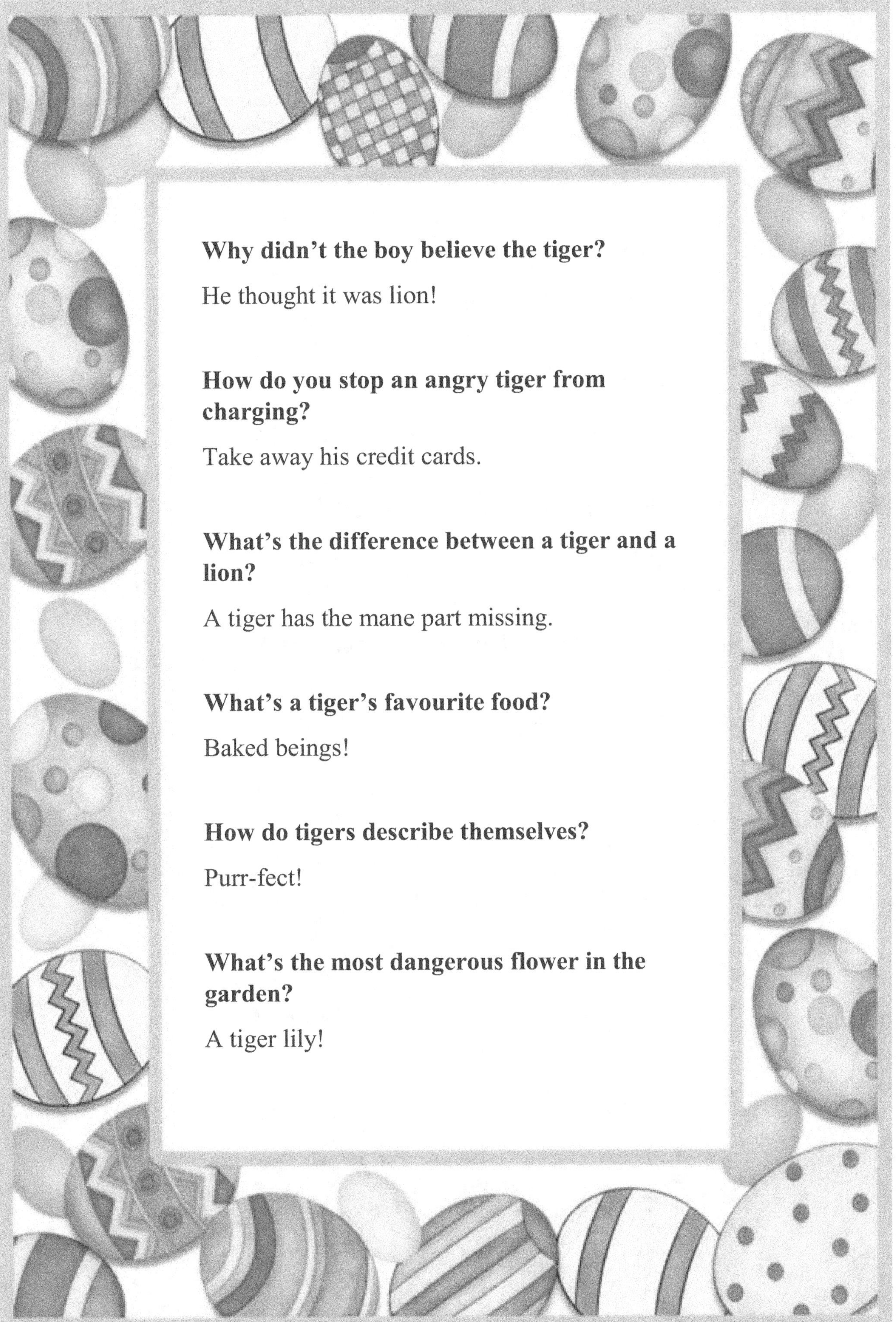

Why didn't the boy believe the tiger?

He thought it was lion!

How do you stop an angry tiger from charging?

Take away his credit cards.

What's the difference between a tiger and a lion?

A tiger has the mane part missing.

What's a tiger's favourite food?

Baked beings!

How do tigers describe themselves?

Purr-fect!

What's the most dangerous flower in the garden?

A tiger lily!

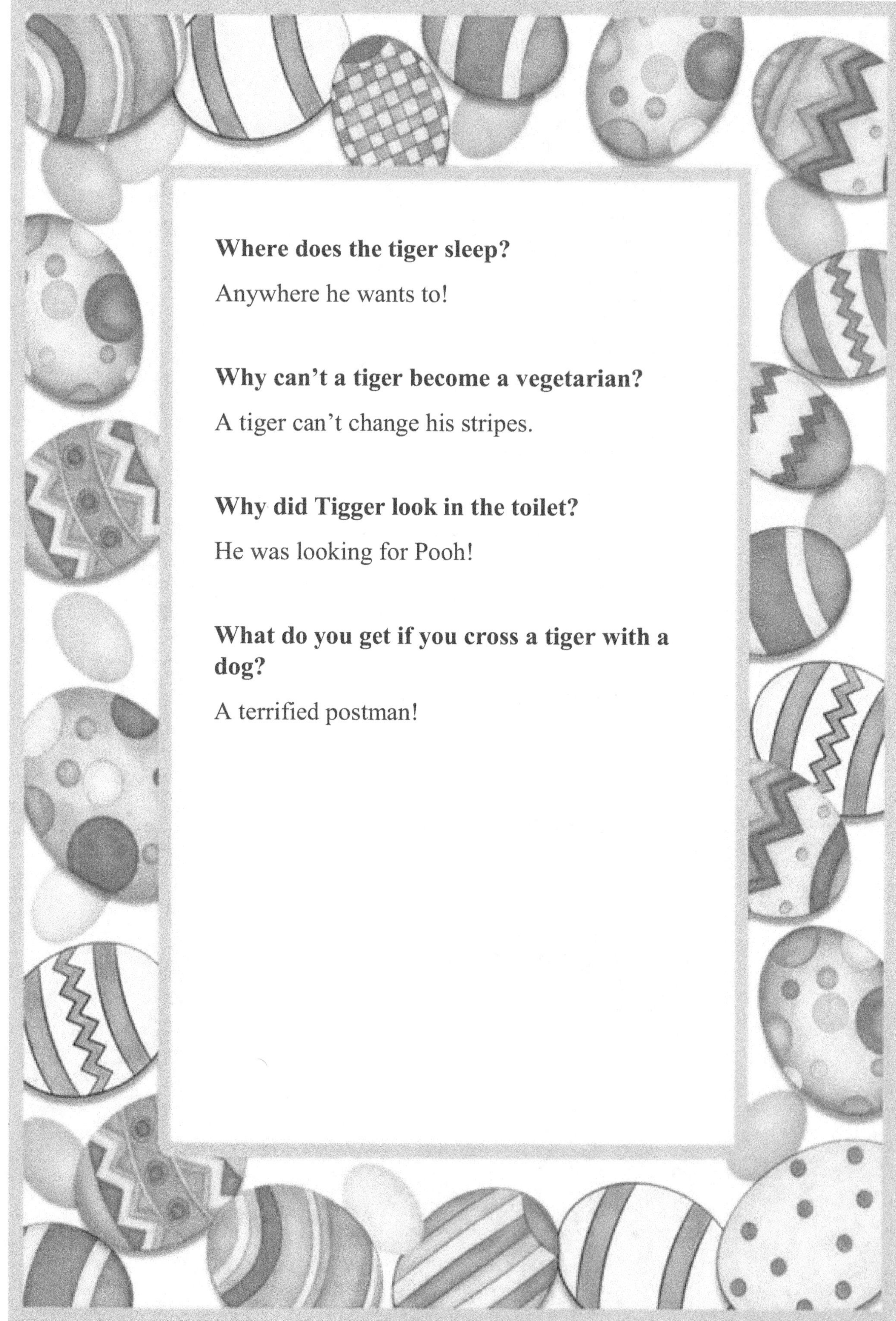

Where does the tiger sleep?

Anywhere he wants to!

Why can't a tiger become a vegetarian?

A tiger can't change his stripes.

Why did Tigger look in the toilet?

He was looking for Pooh!

What do you get if you cross a tiger with a dog?

A terrified postman!

Bear Jokes

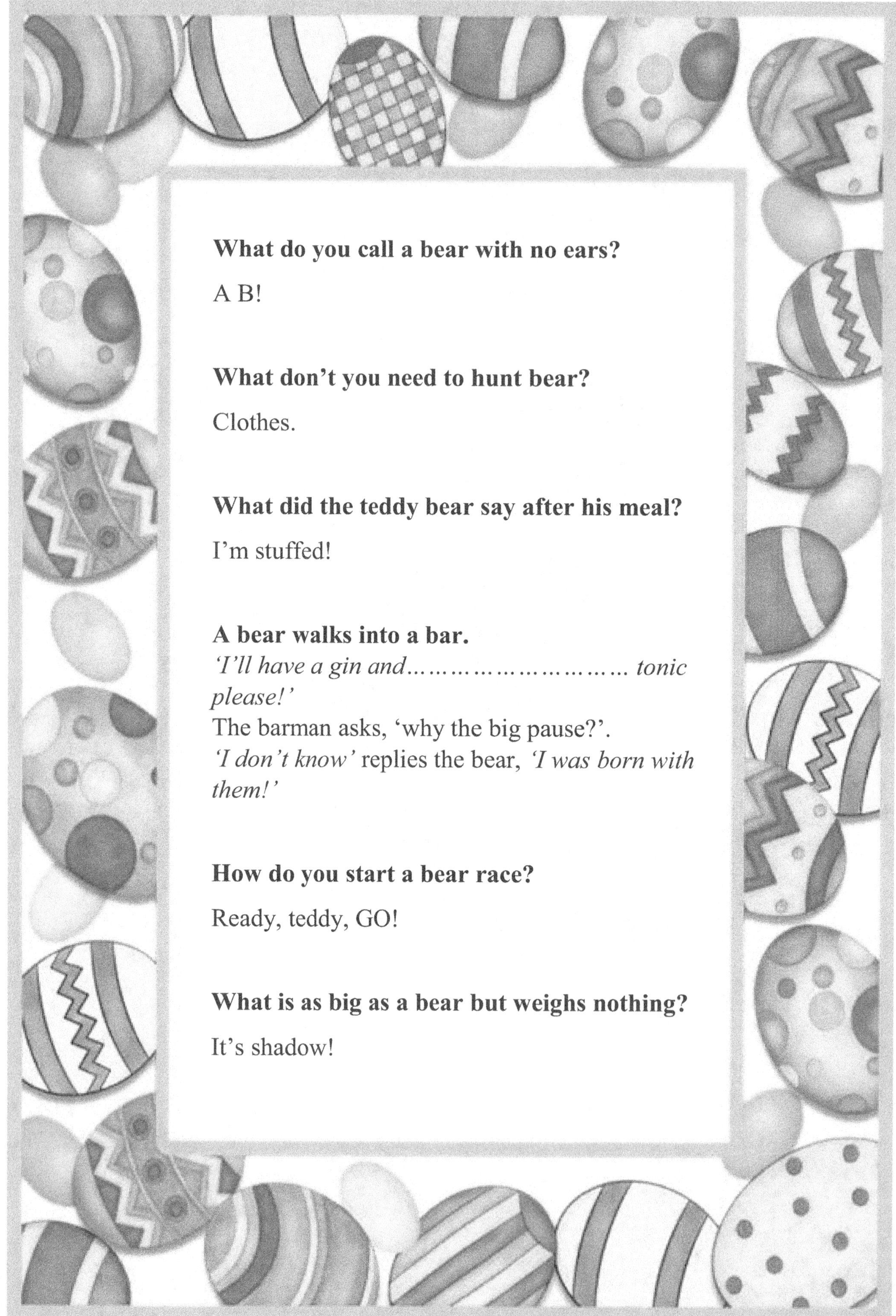

What do you call a bear with no ears?
A B!

What don't you need to hunt bear?
Clothes.

What did the teddy bear say after his meal?
I'm stuffed!

A bear walks into a bar.
'I'll have a gin and………………………. tonic please!'
The barman asks, 'why the big pause?'.
'I don't know' replies the bear, *'I was born with them!'*

How do you start a bear race?
Ready, teddy, GO!

What is as big as a bear but weighs nothing?
It's shadow!

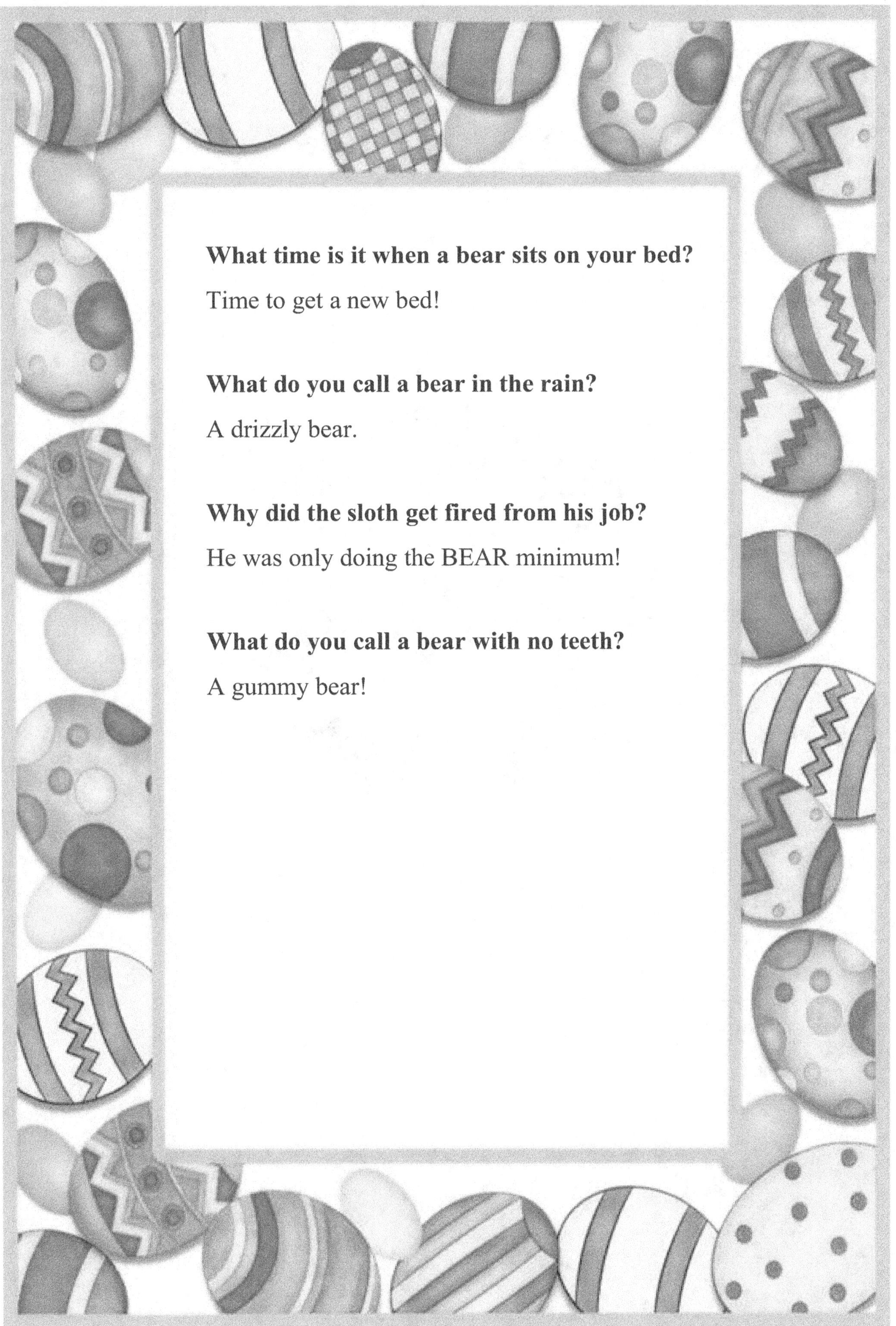

What time is it when a bear sits on your bed?

Time to get a new bed!

What do you call a bear in the rain?

A drizzly bear.

Why did the sloth get fired from his job?

He was only doing the BEAR minimum!

What do you call a bear with no teeth?

A gummy bear!

Insect Jokes

Name the Ant who always likes to be alone?

Independ-ant!

What is the biggest ant in the world?

An eleph-ant!

How do bees brush their hair?

With a honeycomb!

Who comes to a picnic but is never invited?

Ants.

What do you call a bug that jumps over cups?

A glasshopper!

How did the police get rid of the bugs?

They called a SWAT team!

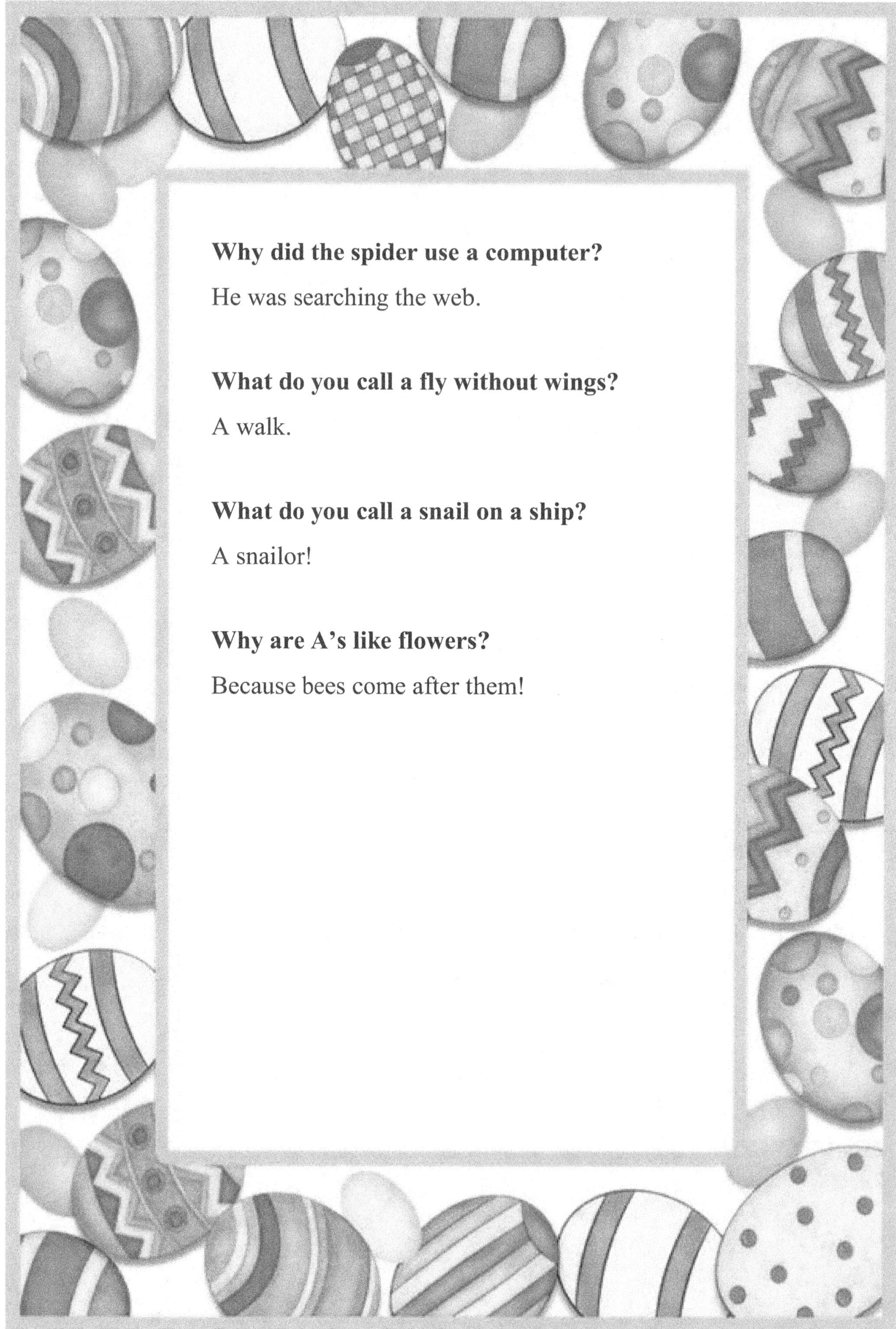

Why did the spider use a computer?

He was searching the web.

What do you call a fly without wings?

A walk.

What do you call a snail on a ship?

A snailor!

Why are A's like flowers?

Because bees come after them!